NO-NONSENSE PR

Based on *Hype Yourself* by Lucy Werner

First published in Great Britain by Practical Inspiration Publishing, 2024

© Lucy Werner and Practical Inspiration Publishing, 2024

The moral rights of the author have been asserted

ISBN 978-1-78860-679-0 (print)
 978-1-78860-681-3 (epub)
 978-1-78860-680-6 (Kindle)

All rights reserved. This book, or any portion thereof, may not be reproduced without the express written permission of the publisher.

Every effort has been made to trace copyright holders and to obtain their permission for the use of copyright material. The publisher apologizes for any errors or omissions and would be grateful if notified of any corrections that should be incorporated in future reprints or editions of this book.

Want to bulk-buy copies of this book for your team and colleagues? We can customize the content and co-brand *No-Nonsense PR* to suit your business's needs.

Please email info@practicalinspiration.com for more details.

Practical Inspiration Publishing

Contents

Series introduction iv

Introduction 1

Day 1: Goal-setting 7

Day 2: Audience 18

Day 3: Avoiding a crisis 25

Day 4: Your media toolkit 31

Day 5: The press release 43

Day 6: Building your PR contacts 52

Day 7: Traditional PR press office 65

Day 8: Raise your profile and personal brand 90

Day 9: Being creative ('brain farts') 98

Day 10: Non-traditional PR 113

All the other days: Onwards and upwards 125

Conclusion 132

Series introduction

Welcome to *6-Minute Smarts*!

This is a series of very short books with one simple purpose: to introduce you to ideas that can make life and work better, and to give you time and space to think about how those ideas might apply to *your* life and work.

Each book introduces you to ten powerful ideas, but ideas on their own are useless – that's why each idea is followed by self-coaching questions to help you work out the 'so what?' for you in just six minutes of exploratory writing. Because that's where the magic happens.

Whatever you're facing, there's a *6-Minute Smarts* book just for you. And once you've learned how to coach yourself through a new idea, you'll be smarter for life.

Find out more...

Introduction

So what do you know about public relations (PR)? Not much, perhaps – other than the bad press it gets!

What is PR?

PR is more than just telling your story to journalists. It's anything you do that's in the public eye, and I believe it's the best free tool you can include in your marketing mix. Unlike advertising, where you're only visible for as long as you pay to be, publicity doesn't expire.

Any time you're responding in the public eye you have an opportunity to hype yourself, whether that's talking to new people at events, responding to a crisis, posting on social media, launching a product, getting people to sign up for emails, promoting awareness for your business or company blog, writing a report or doing speaking engagements.

A great publicist will work with you to help you strategically steer all of this as well as generate creative campaigns to get your message out there.

What PR is not!

One of the biggest mistakes I see is people thinking that PR is writing a press release and issuing it to a contacts list, what's known in the industry as 'spray and pray'. Just, no. PR is not:

- An opportunity for you to tell a journalist what to write – for example, a whole one-page feature on your business saying how great/different/new/unique it is.
- A paid-for promotional or marketing piece of copy (that's an advert).
- All about the contacts in your address book (obviously this helps, but some of the best pieces of coverage I've secured were through bespoke and tailored emails and doing my research).
- An excuse to take a journalist out for a long lunch and get them drunk enough to write

about you (we're not living in a Wolf of Wall Street era, my friends).

The grey area in between

Some people argue that social media/influencer engagement is part of the PR mix, some people see it as a specialist skill, and yet others think it's the job of digital marketing agencies. Whatever your view, it needs to be part of your PR toolkit, so we'll spend some time learning the ropes on this.

Search engine optimization (SEO)/website design/branding – again, there are specialist agencies that focus on each of these elements and some PR agencies also offer this service. And again, what I'll say is that, if you haven't considered these, then with the best PR in your world you'll struggle to get as much traction. If someone can't understand what you're about just from your branding and website, then consider investing in this before hyping yourself.

Why do I need this book?

We're inundated by branding, advertising and companies pushing us to purchase. If Brexit or Donald

Trump taught us anything, it's that consumers make decisions based on emotions, not statistics.

Consumers engage with the people behind brands because it helps them understand how the brand fits with their own identity. When you share who you are and what you're about, you don't even need to sell to your audience any more because they've bought into you.

Below are just some of the ways that publicity could help you:

- If you're not easily searchable it can affect your sales, as people can't find you. But an effective PR campaign will drive up your SEO and make you more visible.
- Acquiring new customers is expensive! Publicity can help you reach a larger audience in a more authentic and engaging way.
- With millions of businesses out there you need to keep front of mind: The successful businesses we remember have founders who understand (or understood) the importance of publicity – think Richard Branson, Steve Jobs, Brené Brown.
- PR-ing yourself means you're forced to constantly evolve, which is the foundation of all business success – in creating new content

to promote your business, you keep yourself informed and your ideas fresh.
- If you're not part of the conversation, then no one will see what you're doing – shout loudly!
- It's cheaper to retain customers than to find new ones.

I always think of PR as like a marathon, because it takes practice, showing up and consistency. If you were a running novice, you'd be seeking advice on which running shoes to buy and following a training programme. Yes, you can just put shoes on and run, and for some people this works out all right, but to avoid injury, insult and to be the absolute best you can be, you have to put the work in.

What do I need?

- A notebook to complete all the tasks and write your answers to the prompt questions.
- A red pen (time to be your own teacher...).
- A 12-month wall chart to mark your key PR events.
- A good relationship with your local newsagent so that you can call in niche magazines when

needed – it's advisable to have an account so you can buy magazines in bulk.

You're ready to start. Over the next ten chapters (ten days, if you fancy treating this as a mini-course) you're going to discover ten key principles of no-nonsense PR, and experiment with using them for yourself.

Let's go!

Day 1
Goal-setting

I'm always amazed how many people carry out PR campaigns with no overarching strategy and focus instead on getting into a publication that they think makes them look good.

Let's start your PR education by getting clear on your business objectives so that all your planned PR activity is aligned. Changing the goals halfway through a campaign means you may have to start from scratch, so it's vital that your business targets are clear, and ideally set out on one page so you can keep referring to them.

Today, let's look at business goals, communication goals and what we have lined up for the next 12 months, to make sure that we don't get lost in the tactics of the day-to-day grind.

Business goals

Where should you start? The following sample objectives and goals might help...

Turnover or business growth

I want to increase revenue streams from consultancy to coaching, books, teaching, courses and products and increase turnover by 50%.

Internal goals

I want to establish an email marketing database and grow my existing social media channels by 200%.

Operational

I want to review effectiveness of current suppliers and contracts.

Industry/customer awareness

I want to grow my profile as a PR expert for small businesses and entrepreneurs to underpin the above goals.

Goal-setting

Communication goals

Your business objectives give you an end goal, so now it's now time to dig deeper into the voice you'll use to hype yourself to get there. The best relationships are based on truth, and in order to hype your business in line with the objectives you just identified, we need to figure out the voice of the true you.

But who *is* the true you? Think about the following questions and examples:

- Are you trying to establish yourself as a voice of authority? In what area?
- Are you an entertainer?
- Do you want to be a quirky, fun brand? Or are you trying to educate consumers about a new product category?
- Do you need to educate people in order to explain your business offering?
- What's unique to your business personality?
- Can you describe your tone of voice?
- Do the adjectives you come up with reflect your true personality?

Examples

Here's how I might describe myself, drawing together my business objectives and my communication objectives:

- I would like to be a no-nonsense industry expert – friendly but direct.
- I want to be honest by sharing business vulnerabilities and lessons learned on the journey.
- I want to lead by example, demonstrating how I use PR to amplify my business.

Tips

- Take some time to really think about your communications objectives.
- Check these against your business objectives – are they a good fit, or do you need to rethink?
- How do you speak? Look back at some of your recent writing or listen to yourself speaking to make sure what you're aiming for is authentically 'you'.

Goal-setting

What motivates you?

Why did you choose your business objectives, and how have you come to the decision that you want to communicate them in the way you've just described? Perhaps you can relate to some of the examples given below. Make sure you're honest with yourself about your real personal and professional motivations as to what drives you to do what you do.

Examples

Here's how I might articulate my business objectives in my own communication style:

- I want to support small businesses because I believe you shouldn't need a big agency budget to access global agency thinking.
- I created a newsletter membership because I love PR and want to share my knowledge to help other business owners learn how to promote their own services.
- I care about independent businesses because I believe they'll leave the world a better place.
- A work/life balance is important to me and this is true for many independent businesses too.

- I want to build a business where I spend less time being busy and more time on delivering publicity advice that has big impact for individuals.
- Having enough time and money was always an issue in my house as a child. I want to build a business that means I have the time to look after myself and my family.

How do you communicate your uniqueness?

What instantly makes every business different is the individuals that are behind it. What makes you and your business different – what are the unique selling points (USPs)? There's no such thing as a new idea but every person has their own 'thumbprint'.

- Make a list of USPs and put an asterisk against any of the things that only you can say (and not your competitors).
- What's your signature style? Are you extremely strategic, funny, creative, practical, understated? List the words that describe your approach.
- Using all of the above, create sentences that are short, clear and concise and easily understandable.

- Cross-reference against your competitor. If they can be applied, go back to the drawing board.

Communications calendar

Plan your year. It will make your content marketing much more effective.

Map out the next 12 months and plot key moments in your year ahead. Internal dates could include: your business's birthday, new employees starting, an annual charity day, launching a new product or service. External dates could be moments happening outside your business that you can tap into, such as industry events, conferences, a 'national' day that's relevant to your business, or attending award ceremonies. Think regionally as well – lots of local regions have their own independent business or founder awards.

Where do you have gaps throughout the year? This could provide you with a moment to try some proactive pitches or launch a few creative ideas on a budget.

Goal-setting

How much time can you dedicate to PR? I'm often asked how much time it takes to do it right, and, to be honest, it's a bit like answering how long is a piece of string. I only use PR to build my business, so I spend a significant part of my time promoting rather than just working in the business.

Think about what needs to be promoted. Break down the business goals by quarter or month. Can you set some tangible goals against that?

Tips

- Plan in advance.
- Start with monthly or quarterly content.
- Write a week-by-week plan at the beginning of each month to keep your strategy on track.
- Schedule a monthly communications planning meeting with yourself to cross-reference against your objectives and stay on brand.
- Keep your business objectives brief and to the point.
- A business goal shouldn't read like an essay. Make it achievable!

Goal-setting

- A measurable goal means that everyone who is working on the business is heading in the same direction.
- Double-check that your business objectives also fit your personal objectives.
- Put your business goals in a place where you can see them. Review them regularly and keep track of which PR activity is aligning with the biggest growth.

✏️ So what? Over to you...

1. What are my most important objectives for PR?

2. Pick the objective that feels most significant. Why is this so important for my business?

Goal-setting

3. How can I break down these goals into monthly or quarterly targets?

Day 2

Audience

You need to know your audience as well as you know yourself and make sure that your promotional efforts are done for them rather than you.

It's all very well getting featured on podcasts, TV, newspapers and radio, or collaborating with an influencer with millions of followers, but if it's not the right target audience then it won't move the dial.

Who is your ideal customer? Try creating an imaginary persona for your ideal client; keeping that person at front of mind will keep your communications on track. Once you know who they are, you can figure out how to reach them.

Audience

Who is your target audience?

How old are they? Where do they live? Who do they live with? What are their hobbies? Can you sketch them or cut out a picture from a magazine to help you visualize them? It can help to give your persona a name, to make them feel more 'real'!

Where are your audience?

Do they watch YouTube? Are they reading magazines? Where do they get their news from? What influences their purchasing decisions? What are their preferred social media channels? Do they read traditional print media, or do they prefer broadcast?

Think about your specific target audience and the different target media they consume. Below is a summary of my two different audiences:

Target group 1

- Solopreneurs/small businesses – mix of urban and rural dwellers, using shared workspaces, attending a lot of panel events. Aged between 30 and 50, equal male/female split. Creative freelance parents, sole traders or creative networking groups.

- Media: *Courier Magazine*, *Wired*, *Forbes*, *Freelance Magazine*, Monocle Entrepreneurs, Secret Leaders, Enterprise Nation, Small Business Britain, ParentsinBiz, DIFTK (Doing it for the Kids), Being Freelance.

Target group 2

- Event programmers, community managers, brand partnership directors, creative programmers.
- Media: LinkedIn, The Do Lectures, The Futur, Creative Meetings, Cannes Lions International Festival of Creativity, Offf festival, Adobe MAX.

Now that you know a bit more about your audience, can you do some research work to build a media mind map?

Create a poll or use ChatGPT as a publicity assistant to brief on the type of audience you have and ask it to help you find a list of media outliers that could work for you. Once you have this list, you can then use it as the basis for researching and locating the specific columns that could work for you.

Tips

- The more specific you can be, the easier it will be to reach your audience; don't be afraid to niche your targeting – it's really effective.
- If you're not sure what media they consume or want to get a better idea, just ask them. Try a simple research exercise on surveymonkey.com, perhaps offering an incentive to encourage participants to help you.
- Don't let your ego distract you from your business objectives; being in an industry publication might win you points, but does it actually increase your target audience?
- Spend some time with your target audience and understand where they're playing.

✏️ So what? Over to you…

1. What surprised you about your target customer as you did this work?

Audience

2. How many target markets do you have, and which are most important to reaching your business goals?

3. Where do you think would be the most effective way to reach them?

Day 3
Avoiding a crisis

When you put your business out there, there are going to be people who like you... and there will inevitably be some who don't. In the age of social media, trolls, unfortunately, are everywhere.

The most important lesson in the heat of the moment is to never get caught up in reacting emotionally. The way to avoid that is to take some time doing preparation work on your business now.

Your most important job is your current customers. They're your most valuable asset. Think about any issues you may have heard from them to date. What are the problems that have arisen? What would be the worst thing for a client to say to you?

If you do find yourself on the receiving end of negative feedback or publicity, it's useful to have some materials prepared in advance to mitigate it blowing up. No matter how big or small your business is, put a crisis Q&A crib sheet together. I know the word crisis can sound scary. This is just the safety procedure in the unlikely event that you do need it, so that you know what to do. Jot down a list of issues that could come up:

- My product was lost in the post.
- It doesn't look like what was advertised.
- The service I received was bad.
- I can't log in.
- I didn't like it /didn't think it was good.

What to do if a crisis hits

Don't panic, and don't hide away. Your Q&A framework is great for forming the basis of your responses but you don't want to sound like a robot.

It's perfectly okay to use a holding note if you need to investigate further and update later. The other point to remember is that a complaint or something going wrong can give us a real opportunity to improve and even strengthen our relationship with our customer.

Avoiding a crisis

Tips

- Don't just ignore customers' or journalists' requests for a response.
- Update your social media as soon as information is available – even if that's just a holding note.
- If you're feeling like you'll react emotionally, consider working with a freelancer to support you in the crisis response. This will help you pre-empt disasters and also give you more confidence in dealing with them.
- Write down all the negative questions or statements that could crop up and how you might respond.

✏️ So what? Over to you…

1. Where are you most at risk of/have you already experienced negative feedback?

Avoiding a crisis

2. Where might your business be most at risk?

3. What practical steps can you take now to prevent a crisis?

Day 4

Your media toolkit

It's now time to look at the essentials you need before you speak to media, event organizers, brand partners, sponsorship or collaborators.

I recommend you create a folder – called 'press' or 'media toolkit' – where you save all the documents you need for your press and marketing purposes, and that you update them regularly.

Let's look at all the elements you need to have in place before you start your campaign.

- One-liner
- Biography
- Business biography boiler plate
- Images

One-liner

The people you remember best are those who tell you what they do clearly and concisely.

Nailing your summary sentence is a key skill, and it should roll off the tongue. Just as you know the hospital you were born in, your date of birth and your mother's maiden name, you need to be able to reel off what your business does with confidence and in a pithy way.

- How would you describe what your business does in one sentence, say, when you're chatting with a friend?
- Write a paragraph to explain what your business does but then chop out all unnecessary words.
- Test it out on someone who doesn't know you – do they 'get it' or are they still mystified?

A good example of a personal one-liner: 'I'm Lucy Werner and I help founders get famous.'

A bad example of a personal one-liner: 'I'm Lucy Werner and I am an innovative, disruptive creative, multi-hyphen small business owner who helps mission-led purposeful brands and gets them out there through hype in courses, coaching, workshops books and education.'

Your media toolkit

The latter is rather long and over-wordy, making it harder to digest.

Tips

Your one-liner is *not* your USP. It's what I call the 'Ronseal-plus intrigue' to describe what it is your brand does; it needs to be clear but still leave an element of curiosity, so people want to know more.

- Keep it super simple; we're looking for 10–12 words here *max*, people.
- Check all your social media accounts and your website – are you using the same information across all platforms?
- Practise saying your one-liner out loud. Does it sound like you? Adjust as necessary!

Boiler plate

This should look like a potted history of your business and is information that rarely changes – it's often used at the bottom of a press release, newsletter, underneath a pitch email to press and broadcast or business about pages.

The term originates from the early 1900s when widely syndicated newspaper stories were supplied to local presses with the text already set up and ready to print on steel plates that resembled those used to make steam boilers. It became shorthand for any standard copy, such as a business biography.

- What actually *is* your business? You need a brief statement on what the business does and, crucially, the name of your business.
- Where does your business do this, and since when?
- Who established the business and for what purpose?
- Are there any notable business successes to highlight?

Tips

- Make your boiler plate short, sharp and succinct!
- Show it to someone who doesn't know anything about your business and make sure that they can read it and understand what your business does.
- Cut out any words or language you don't need.
- It should be a factual, pithy marketing paragraph, so avoid opinionated or emotive language.

Your media toolkit

Images

One of the best investments I can recommend is to splash out on some professional photography. With great photography you instantly elevate your personal and business brand and you'll need to get the return on the investment, which forces you to use them.

Founder images

The press shots of yourself are essential for:

- Snatching extra space in a newspaper feature
- Guest panellists at a conference
- Award entries
- Guest posts
- Updating your social media channels, including on your website
- Podcast promotion.

Getting the right image

- Work with a photographer you feel comfortable with. All portrait photographers have a different style.
- Look around your network and ask for recommendations. It's not always about going with the cheapest photographer.

No-Nonsense PR

- Create a mood board of the style of photography you like; for example, on Pinterest to share as part of the briefing process.
- Pick a photographer who provides a briefing template, or who at least sends through some questions in advance of the shoot.

Tips

- Aim for at least six to eight headshots on plain backgrounds.
- Request a mixture of landscape and portrait (increasingly I find I need to provide landscape profile pictures for blog posts/media articles).
- On shoot day wear a few outfits, with different colours/levels of formality.
- Ensure you have professional cropped head and shoulder shots.
- Ask your photographer to send images to you in both hi- and low-res.
- A hi-res 300 dpi (dots per inch) jpeg format is best for the majority of print media/marketing requirements.

Your media toolkit

Product photography

Most media want products on a ghost or white background that they can cut out easily for their shopping pages.

- Make sure you have a selection of shots that can be used for media.
- Don't overthink it! Businesses are often scared of the simplicity of shooting on a plain white background, but trust me when I say that this is the most requested shot I'm ever asked for. These days, with design tools, we can easily remove a background, but we still want the best quality possible.

Tips

- If it's a product shot, shoot it flat on a white background (sometimes called a ghost cut-out).
- Don't sent imagery as email attachments to press contacts – you'll clog up their inbox.
- Have a downloadable image library where you can send anyone who's asking for an image.

Biographies

'Can you send me their bio?' That's what journalists always ask publicists when they're considering running a story on a client – and they want it immediately.

A bio should be one of the first assets you create for your media toolkit. To begin with, write down everything. Not only is this a useful way to uncover all your forgotten talents and experience, but it may also unearth something different that you can build on. Ask yourself the following questions:

- What skills do I have that are relevant to this business?
- What are my relevant academic or professional qualifications?
- What's my industry experience?
- Any other strengths to highlight?
- Do I have a quirky hobby and/or habit?

The red pen

Rank the different points by relevancy. Then start your cull of what might be irrelevant for your first draft. (Keep a long-form version of everything for future use and to keep updating.)

Your media toolkit

What's your name and where do you come from?

Start simply and with the basics – your name and where you currently work, or some examples of who you currently work for, if you're freelance.

Add a personal detail

People relate better to people who are personable, so consider adding an interesting tidbit. It gives the reader something to care about.

Keep it succinct

Absolutely no more than 250 words (bonus points if you can keep it below 150 words). If you start putting too much information down, it actually distracts from you as an expert. People don't remember long bios, they get bored by them. You can always link to your website to encourage people to find out more.

Tips

- Your bio is *not* a one-size-fits-all template – allow it to evolve depending on which platform or business is using it.

- Practise saying your biography out loud. Does it sound like you? Adjust as necessary!
- Check your master biography at least once a year to ensure all recent developments are included.
- Include a link to download your bio and images from your website to encourage people to book you as a speaker.
- Have you also drafted bio options for social media, optimized for each platform's style and extent?

So what? Over to you…

1. Thinking back over everything you've read about here, what's the most important element of your media toolkit to focus on right now?

Your media toolkit

2. What's the first step towards putting that in place?

3. How will you go about getting high-quality images of yourself and making them easily accessible upon request?

Day 5

The press release

I hate press releases. Or rather, I hate how they're used.

Many business owners (and even some PRs) wrongly think that publicity is about writing a press release and sending it to all your contacts. This is lazy and sloppy: it's like cold-calling a business to sell to them without knowing a single thing about them or whether your product or service is even useful.

Press releases are useful because they provide crucial background information for a journalist to write an informed article – but writing a press release and sending it out is *not* PR. What you actually need is a well-tailored pitch supported by a press release (we'll come on to how you put a pitch together in Day 6).

But let's start with the basics: what *is* a press release? It's simply a one- or two-page document that shares your business's breaking news. When done right they can be crucial for driving media coverage and building brand awareness and they're a cost-effective way to market your business (they only cost you a bit of time).

Examples of when you might want to issue a press release include:

- Breaking news announcements
- Events
- Partnerships or collaborations
- Product launches or limited editions
- Sharing research
- Announcing award wins of senior hires
- Crisis management.

Structuring your press release

Headline

Use an attention-grabbing headline. It can include a pun, but make sure it's clear what it's about. Think about the headlines of articles in the paper when you read them: check your headline for readability using a

The press release

tool such as 'headline analyser'. Successful headlines draw you in.

Date and location

Include your location and the date that the press release is being issued for.

Introduction

This first paragraph should set the scene and tone for the whole press release. This first paragraph is your opening for setting the story. It should be very clear what the news hook is within this paragraph. Start with the five Ws:

1. Who is this story about?
2. What is happening?
3. Where is it going on?
4. When will it occur?
5. Why is it important?

Paragraphs two to five

These should include the other details of your story in a descending order of importance. For now, keep all information about when you were founded, what you do, team biographies and other factual information out of the press release. (That isn't to say that the rest of your release shouldn't be factual; it absolutely must be factual and objective.) The next several paragraphs should tell the complete story concisely, with important supporting details included.

Style: other things to watch out for

Ditch the jargon! Or at least make sure you don't have too much of it. Ask a friend if they understand what you're saying. If they find it boring or complicated, rework it.

Quotes

Include a quote from the CEO/founder to give context but don't use clichéd quotes such as 'I am delighted to announce...' Who actually talks like that?

Your quote needs to be bold. Make sure it gives a purpose. It's your opportunity to give more colour or opinion and can be really personal. Make it memorable. (Make sure you attribute the quote, and make it clear who is saying what and why.)

The press release

Press contact

Include contact information – your name, email and a phone number. The phone number is key, particularly if time is of the essence and a journalist needs to be able to fact check. (If it's your personal mobile number, make sure your phone accepts calls from unknown numbers for the next few days at least!) Key URLs and social media handles should also be shared here.

Editors' notes

Key prices, dates, event information or any other information that can be included in listicle format.

Boiler plate

The boiler plate you crafted earlier should sit right at the bottom of your press release.

Tips

- Keep a press release on file that explains what you do as a background document for practice or in case a journalist requests one.
- Listicles combine the depth of an article but in the style of a list.

- If your business isn't well known, maybe consider not using it for your headline and think instead what the headline of the story might be.
- The press release should be written in the same style as a news article – in that the news is right up top and in front and the supporting background information comes further down.
- Don't overdo it – avoid overuse of exclamation marks, fluffy language or wild claims; for example, 'the World's First' or 'Best New Product for XX'.
- Check your spelling and grammar!
- Keep longer factual information for the editors' notes section at the bottom.
- Keep the press release to less than one side of A4 – keep it short and to the point.

Putting a press release together is one job, but if it's going to be effective you really need to know where you intend to place it. My advice is to send it in the body of an email underneath a well-tailored pitch email – see Day 6 for more on this. Never attach it, and make sure it's readable within the email. *Now* you're reaching people.

The press release

So what? Over to you…

1. How – if at all – are you using press releases at the moment?

2. Think of something significant happening in your business at the moment or in the near future and write a brief press release you can use to help you pitch the story to journalists.

The press release

3. What boilerplate copy can you create and keep on hand so you're ready to pitch in future?

Day 6
Building your PR contacts

In order to know who you might want to be sending that press release or tailored pitch to, let's have a look at what types of journalists there are.

You've created the foundation of your PR campaign, so now let's look at how to start your press office by thinking about these 'how to' points:

- Understanding different journalists
- How to build your media database
- How you can build your relationships with media

Understanding different types of journalists

A key challenge I see working with small business owners and solopreneurs is that they want a list of 'editors to email'. This is why I don't advocate for using media lists – this is spam. Instead of thinking 'I need a list of editors', think more precisely: what are the five exact columns or pages you want to appear in? Who writes them? Yes, this takes a lot of work, but remember: if you were paying for an advertisement it would cost you thousands.

Before you start pitching, let me introduce you to the various different types of journalists.

Opinion editor

This is perhaps a misnomer – they're interested in writing by sourcing others' unique voices rather than their own.

Commercial content editor

This is a paid-for partnership between yourself and the brand, and prices range for print and digital. Brand partnerships need to be well-matched in order to be effective. However, there are often opportunities for brands looking for case studies, which could give you a free opportunity for premium coverage.

Freelance writer

Freelance writers generally write for publications and brands and pitch their stories to commissioning editors. So sending a press release to a freelance writer is unlikely to get picked up unless they write news and it's a crucial breaking news story.

Kate Hollowood is a freelance writer who offers some useful tips:

> 'Fit the bill... don't waste your time if you can't meet [the journalist's requirements].'

> 'Stand out in your initial email... explain how your case study fits the requirements they are looking for. Then include a few sentences about how your case study is uniquely interesting.'

> 'Flattery gets you nowhere... branded content is about telling an interesting story rather than shouting about how amazing the company is...'

Staff writer

Kathryn Wheeler is staff writer at *Happiful* magazine; she explained to me what her role means:

'I work so broadly across the magazine, the main thing that I'm looking for from pitches is that they are offering something that I couldn't already do myself, or don't have time to do myself.'

'... strong imagery is incredibly important – it can be the difference between a piece making it through or not.'

Digital writer

Sarah Orme is the digital editor for calmmoment.com:

'I'm always trying to create interesting articles that cover our key topics: wellbeing, mindfulness, living, creating and escaping. I'm always looking for people who have expertise in a wellness-related field who are happy to share their knowledge. I really like it when people have done their research and approach me with potential article ideas that they might be able to help with.'

'[Don't send] pre-written articles, it's much quicker and easier to send ideas!'

News editor

Sarah Drumm is a freelance journalist:

> 'We are looking for stories that are new, exciting and have an element of urgency around them.'
>
> 'News editors and reporters sometimes have the reputation that they are hunting for scandals and missteps but we are equally keen to hear from companies who have launched exciting innovations, overhauled their business models, or overcome a huge challenge.'

Editor

Joe Makertich (editor of *TimeOut London*):

> 'The best editors manage to imbue their publication with a... vibe that's their own. They do this not by micromanaging every aspect of the production (although sometimes this is tempting) but by enabling each member of staff. Once each member of staff, no matter how junior, feels valued by the editor, the

publication begins to sing... good stories all need interest/drama/jeopardy.'

'Go straight to staff writers and try and build a relationship. In other places it would be the features editor or front-section editor. In an ideal world you'd know the way each publication functioned. Who commissions who? Where do the ideas come from? Who's the person in constant need of stories/people/products?'

Broadcast contacts

Presenter

The presenter's role is just that, to present. They don't get involved with the production and creation of the show's content. So leave them in peace; they can't help you.

Forward planner

Unsurprisingly, these people forward plan a show's content. Send a note to forward planners a few weeks in advance to get in the diary, and then perhaps follow up the week before to give them a heads up of the story to see whether it fits any slots they have that week.

Digital producer

A digital producer means the person who is responsible for creating content for social channels associated with the show and in fact might even create a completely different bunch of content to the television show.

Demo producer

The person whose responsibility it is to source products that will be demoed on the show.

Celebrity bookers

You may very well want to pitch your story to a celebrity booker who is charged with inviting stars to appear for 'on the sofa'-type pieces. Nice work if you can get it!

Beauty/fashion producer

For beauty or fashion products, make contact with either the beauty or fashion producers of the shows you wish to appear on.

How to build your media database

The small business owners who become the go-to experts aren't the ones with contacts, they're the ones who are passionate about telling their story and taking the time to craft it right rather than rushing it.

I keep notes of media that are relevant to me or my clients and include their first name and surname, their publication, their job title, name of their column, their email address, any background information, social media handles and phone number (although as a general rule of thumb, don't phone them unless it's critical breaking news).

X/Twitter

You should by now have the right name of the journalist you need – check X (formerly known as Twitter), as most journalists are active here and their bio often reveals how they want to be contacted and/or a contact address or website.

The website of the publication/inside the magazine

Finding the right contact is important. Take the time to study online or in print and you'll start to notice a pattern in who is covering the stories you want to be featured in. You can find the email format of most publications by checking the publication.

How can you build your relationship with media?

Finding opportunities or jumping on the bandwagon of a journalist request is a great way to practise your media relations skills, and it keeps you top of mind for when that perfect opportunity comes along.

Media enquiry databases

It's often worth having a trial of, say, PressPlugs or ResponseSource when you're starting out to get an idea of the sort of different desks and sheer number of journalists that there are. Publicists are all usually subscribed to at *least* one media enquiry databases.

#journorequest

I recommend you have an account on X, if only for press office activity. Search in the tool bar for #journorequest or #haro (help a reporter out) then select latest. Here you'll see a list of requests that are suitable for you.

Building your PR contacts

Lightbulb

A private paid-for Facebook group that's a very inexpensive way to connect directly with media that's for entrepreneurs and journalists. As a business owner you can pitch a story or simply check daily for journalist requests to pitch for. There are no publicists allowed so it's a fantastic place for you to connect directly with media.

Newsletters and podcasts

Want to just start pitching to write for other newsletters, guest workshop for memberships or podcasts? I create a quarterly directory that I email out to paid subscribers of my newsletter. It usually features 50-plus people actively looking for guests like you.

Tips

- Triple-check that you/your product is the right fit for that publication.
- Make sure you're fully answering the brief and give them everything at once – don't make them do more work.

- Time is of the essence. You need to be one of the first to respond, because if the first replies hit the mark, they're unlikely to read any of the others.
- Include your biography, one-liner on your business and a photograph so that they know you're serious.
- If you get featured, give them a thank you. This is *free* exposure for you and it's a great way to maintain your relationship.

So what? Over to you…

1. Which publications and websites do you most want to target for coverage?

2. What kinds of journalists are the most likely to be receptive, and why?

3. How will you build your media database, perhaps just starting with five key journalists?

Day 7

Traditional PR press office

Okay, by now you have all your press material ready, and you've started to understand some of the different opportunities. There are so many different types of columns, pages and sections from travel, property, business, lifestyle, family that could work for you.

Let's get started with a few of my favourite ways to raise a founder's profile to build business awareness. It's a lot easier to place opinions and human-interest stories than it is just to get a write-up about a product or business. Here are some of the best.

Guest posts

For me, one of the most useful tools for any entrepreneur or service business owner is the much-underrated guest post.

Guest posts are often called other things, such as opinion pieces, thought leadership, op-eds, blog posts or 'how to' guides. Guest posting is one of my favourite ways to easily get press:

- A free and repeatable system – once you've nailed how to do this, you have endless opportunities to get your brand out there.
- An opportunity for an alternative income stream.
- A great way to build your credibility and authority, and to cement your position as an expert.
- Useful for tactical placement with brands, other newsletters or influential small business owners who can grow your audience.

What's the difference between an opinion piece and a thought leadership article?

An opinion piece should be just that – your own opinion – ideally the stronger the better! It will

Traditional PR press office

create debate and wider discussion and you'll secure a wider readership and exposure as people 'like' and comment. It's likely to have more of a human-interest element and therefore can create a greater connection with your audience.

A thought leadership piece can encompass opinions but also shows you're a thought leader in this area, so it could be a 'how to' guide or a 'top tips' piece.

- Read: The more information you consume, the more ideas it will spark.
- Niche: Go back to your business objectives, target audience and media. Where are your audience? Are there specialist reports, columns or angles you can look at?
- List build: Start to brainstorm a list of the key areas you want to talk about and continually update and add to it. You can never have too many topic ideas. *But* you do need to stick to a few to give you an area that you're known for.
- Build a list of the titles you'd like to be featured in both personally and professionally for a guest article.
- Use ChatGPT or Google to help you pull out submission guidelines for the titles you'd like to write for.

Here's how I structure my pitch emails:

Read other guest posts and guidelines

- Spend a good hour reading other posts and often the site will have guidelines on how to pitch.
- Know your title before you pitch. I usually start off with a wish list of the top three dream pieces I'd love to get.
- Warning: as an aside, don't write the article first and then look to place it. This is backwards and one size fits no one, my friend.

Subject line

I always write 'Pitch for: Name of column, name of publication and a short headline'. This demonstrates to the journalist immediately that the pitch is tailored to them, you've read the publication and you've crafted something bespoke for them. The headline should be your top pick of an article for them that would grab their readers' attention.

Traditional PR press office

Intro

Keep it friendly (not over-friendly) and to the point. Don't bother with 'How are you today?' – journalists are busy, and you probably don't know them, so just cut to the chase.

> Hello (name – spelled correctly),
>
> My name is XX and I'm an expert in YY and ZZ. Would you be interested in the following ideas for a guest post...?

Article ideas

Suggest two or three ideas; it gives the journalist some brain food and the opportunity to provide feedback and editorial direction. I write one sentence per topic with a maximum of two or three pithy bullet points underneath.

Examples of previous writing

Use links to a blog on your website, LinkedIn or Medium to demonstrate your writing style. Again, I tend to bullet point a few examples.

Demonstrate wider expertise

I include a boiler plate, business bio or personal bio right at the bottom. This provides a wider context and credentials to cement why you might be good for them.

Sign-off

Make sure you have a signature with your email and phone number included. Your email may very well get forwarded on and you want to make sure you're easy to reach.

Tips

- Guest posts shouldn't read like an advertisement for your business. People want to know about your business challenges, interesting points of view, human-interest stories.
- Stick to just three ideas when pitching to a publication.
- Give an example of previous writing you can use to demonstrate.

Features

Two is a coincidence, three is a trend. A feature pitch is you highlighting a trend. This is where knowing your competitors can actually be a great thing.

News and more urgent shorter pieces are up front, and features tend to be around the middle. These are long-form pieces of writing that tend to quote several experts to demonstrate a trend or a debate.

Rather than pitching yourself or your company, a feature pitch can be a way of making you more relevant, because telling your own brand story on its own isn't enough.

I recommend using #journorequest or Lightbulb, as mentioned in the connecting with media section, to respond to an existing feature request, but you could also try a features editor to pitch your own.

Business

- Do you have any interesting HR policies in place?
- Perhaps you work in an unusual way?
- Perhaps you have an alternative recruitment policy?

- What's innovative and unique to how your business operates, whether that's an internal process or your go-to-market proposition?

Customers

- What's interesting about your audience?
- Have you noticed a behavioural change or anything interesting about your audience?
- Have you had to adapt your offering or product to meet customer demand?

Personal

- What's interesting about your personal journey? Have you had to overcome adversity to create your business?
- Have you had an unusual 'lightbulb' moment?
- Do you work with a twin, a best friend, an ex, your grandparents, or is there something unusual or unique about your business set-up?

Examples

Below are six different feature types:

1. **Trends:** for example: 'cleanfluencers'. There have been several articles on people who are cleaning influencers, or the top cleaning/home tidying products.
2. **Seasonal features:** there will be recurrent themes for features that appear, such as a lot of 'end-of-year teacher gifting' features that look at gifts for this time of year.
3. **Getting personal:** people with unusual backgrounds, hobbies or achievements can make interesting stories. Who are the characters of your story and do they fit a particular profile? If you have statistics and research, can you provide a case study that provides an emotive connection?
4. **New consumer behaviour:** the rise of subscriptions, the death of the high street, veganism, the Internet of Things in the home.
5. **Data:** examples of customer data might include shopping peaks after a cultural event, items in the news *or* identify a surprising new trend.

6. **Trade features:** you could contribute to an already existing feature in a trade magazine such as *The Grocer* (which has Forward Feature lists). These break down the topics they're planning to cover, so there are opportunities to pitch comments. This can result in more coverage and awareness about a new product range than a stand-alone press release.

Feature pitch tips

- Make sure you have a calendar date or relevant newshook from the content you've created.
- If you don't have a reason to go 'right now', consider holding on to your pitch until a suitable newshook becomes available.
- Check the features for the media outlet and read through their current format.
- Are you providing assets, offering case studies, quotes from industry experts?
- Do you have any strong photography or infographic data visuals that could accompany the piece?

- Are you ensuring that you're telling the story of a wider industry piece rather than just an article based on yourself?
- Identify the name of the features journalist who is writing about your topic/area. If the name isn't obvious, can you find the name of the commissioning editor or features director?
- Write a clear subject line (not in CAPSLOCK – nobody likes being shouted at) explaining the angle.
- Ensure you give the journalist enough time to provide feedback. Pick *one* journalist to pitch your feature to and tailor it to them. A polite chase once or twice to see if it's relevant is fine but give them some time. If you don't hear back, this is likely to be a no, so allow yourself enough time to take the feature to a few different publications.

Some questions to consider

- What significant dates or consumer behaviour does your business have access to?
- Do you think you've created a market first or are you part of an emerging new category?

- Can you use business data from the City Business Library, for example, or look at Trade Associations to find recent reports and statistics that can support a wider contextual piece that your business could fit into?
- Look at the feature and trend articles in local newspapers to get a feel for the topics being covered: how could you best fit with their angle?

Interviews and Q&As

When I started in PR, the only slots available for business were aimed at corporates with a turnover of £2.5 million-plus. Today, the blurring of the work/life balance, portfolio careerists and the rise of the side-hustlers means the media landscape has changed and there are plenty of opportunities for Q&As.

Size doesn't matter. Repeat. Size doesn't matter. Leave your ego at the door and start small. Look at which business blogs, newsletters, digital publications feature, or interview, business founders in your niche.

Tips

- Check out your business competitors and see where they're being featured – use this to

build a list of niche slots and columns you can pitch for.
- Keep a notebook to hand when you're on Instagram or browsing the net and make sure you note down any relevant columns/bloggers you could work with.
- Cross-reference this interview list with your business objectives, target audience and target media list to make sure you're keeping on brand.
- Look at service industries in your area – for example, many marketing, design and PR agencies I know that focus on small businesses also like to profile small businesses.

Example

On first glance you might think Davinia from Rainchq, whose business is to empower women to invest, could only be profiled for fintech and trade-specific publications. But after revisiting our business objectives and identifying that we wanted to grow her consumer audience, we reimagined her strategy:

> Subject line: 'Founder of fintech service that empowers women to invest for "Mama Meets" column'.

Then in the body of the email I crafted something that's really tailored for that title, for example:

I work with Davinia Tomlinson, founder of Rainchq, a service that empowers women to invest. As well as a fintech juggernaut, she also is the mother of two children, and I thought her start-up story as well as finance tips would be of interest to your readers. Particularly as mothers, we struggle more with the gender pay gap and long-term pension poverty.

Thanks

Lucy [making sure my email and phone number are in my signature]

(Underneath, I'd also include a biography, and either the business boiler plate or a press release as background information.)

TV

There are loads of ways that everyday people can secure exposure on broadcast channels, but does it hit your business objectives?

Traditional PR press office

- Research different shows. Make sure you know exactly which segment it would be suitable for you to be featured in. Know the name of who presents that segment and *spell it right*!
- Once you know which slot works for you, watch it a few times and really get a feel for the style of the segment and content.
- Can you add to your own story and suggest some other brands that it can work with? Could an expert give it more clout?
- Create your media list of relevant producers for the shows that you want to be on.
- Try to send an email as early in the day as possible – at least before 10:00 am.
- Just to reiterate, because it's crucial – your pitch to TV must be visual.
- Draft your expert pitch crib email. If a story breaks, you then only need to amend two bullet points in reaction, and you're ready to go.

Product placement slots

There are many daytime and weekend magazine-style shows such as *This Morning*, *Good Morning Britain* and

Sunday Brunch. Just like a cross between a newspaper and magazine they have a hybrid of slots. There's usually a topical news story/guest on the sofa, perhaps a magazine-style feature that might look at top tips for holiday packing, for example.

Regional newsjacking

If you're working on a local news story, such as a charity event, you should consider going to both your local BBC and ITV local news channels. For a daily regional news programme, you might want to pitch a few days in advance or on the actual day.

Ask the expert

Thanks to the changing media landscape, we have news breaking 24 hours a day and that means experts to comment on news stories are in constant demand. I recommend creating an expert crib sheet that's tailored for broadcast.

If you know something is coming up in the news and you have a point of view on it, such as the budget, look at who has previously written about it. Craft a few bullet points to show what your point of view and opinion could be. Email the journalist with the subject line to show them you're an expert with a timely response. Rather than just your business or personal name, tailor it to what's happening; for example:

- Pitch: finance expert and case study in response to the budget for cohabitors
- Underneath your thoughts, include your biography, photo and contact information so they have everything ready to hand to use.

Using this technique will allow you to become the go-to expert.

Real-life case studies

If you'd like help selling your own personal story to the media, then you could consider approaching a service that sells-in stories themselves to TV and radio and is always on the hunt for interesting stories and often paying guests to be featured.

A note before you appear on TV

- A bit of media training or practising what you want to say can make you less nervous.
- Don't script yourself; by all means rehearse, but you don't want to sound like a robot.

- Think about what the key points are that you want to land and note them down as prompts.
- Don't wear anything too jazzy or too small/tight, or a busy print.
- Make sure you arrange recording of the show that you'll appear on so you can share.

A note after you appear on TV

- Thank the producer/booker for booking you – if you forge a relationship there's a good chance you'll be booked again.
- Cut and share the video clip of you afterwards, and add it to your expert crib sheet to demonstrate your ability on air.
- Put it on your LinkedIn and remind your followers from time to time that you did TV by resharing. You don't need to just use it once.

Tips

- Keep it timely – you don't want to waste your time by going too far in advance or too late in the day.

Traditional PR press office

- If you can't find who to speak to, try calling the switchboard and asking for the right contact email.
- Talk your pitch out loud. What's the real story and can you sell it in with just a few sentences?
- What assets do you have that work for TV? Think about who you're offering as a speaker and what they can talk about. Can you offer a unique location or background that will make filming easy? Remember, TV is visual so you want to be providing ideas for why you/your story could work visually.
- Don't be egocentric.
- Producers care about how the story relates to their audience. So, what's the 'viewer benefit' of you being on TV?

Radio

Radio is not only one of the top media that Brits listen to on a regular basis, but it's seen as one of the most trusted sources. Who wouldn't want to be on one of the topical shows on Radio 4?

- Think about the radio stations your audience would engage with.

- Listen to the actual shows, get a feel for the different presenting styles and chat segments.
- List the programmes/slots that would be relevant for your business and add to the media database you created.
- Review all the guest post and feature ideas you created and think about how these could be applied for radio.
- Are there any relevant calendar dates or national days that you're specifically qualified to speak on?
- Listen to the shows on a regular basis.
- Look for the contact details for the producer of that show.
- You need to ensure that you're contacting the planner, researcher or producer of that show and *not* the presenters.
- Keep your pitch succinct (with correct spellings!).
- Be clear about your story and why it's important.

Here are some great tips from Johnny Seifert, showbiz editor for talkRADIO, producer for the *Badass Women's Hour XL* and host of the *Secure the Insecure* podcast, where he talks to reality stars about their insecurities.

Traditional PR press office

- If you're struggling to find contact details for a show, check media.info for individual contact details or X/Twitter. Most producers will have their email in their X/Twitter bio.
- Keep your pitch succinct, three lines ideally – Dear (insert person's name and spell it correctly). If you spell my name wrong, you don't even get a look-in. Be really clear on what you do and what the story is and a clear reason of why you want to be on, focused on how it will be of interest to our listeners rather than benefit yourself (and make sure you spell the station name correctly).
- I'd recommend not asking for interview questions, because if you rehearse your answers it can lack the emotion when it's a live recording. If you're interested in speaking radio, then there's a good chance you're already an expert in what you speak on, so you won't need to read from a piece of paper.
- Make sure you can own what you say: debates work really well, and we welcome strong opinions, but you can't take it back afterwards. And remember, if a debate we feature goes viral, then it can mean free

advertising for your business. Just make sure it's working for you and your brand.
- If you want to pitch off a national newshook (e.g. World Kindness Day) and you're an expert with something punchy to say about this, then I'd email one week before and again on the day (before 8am) – that's the sort of thing that can easily go on the drive time show, for example.

Tips

- Make sure your ego doesn't block you from pitching for interviews in smaller niche titles.
- Check your competitors or other people in your industry to get ideas of where you could be.
- Think outside the box – I'm in PR but I rarely pitch for PR interview slots; I focus on niches where my audience is.

So what? Over to you…

1. If you were to pitch a guest piece, what might that be and where might you pitch it?

2. If you were to pitch an interview/expert piece, what might that be and where might you pitch it?

3. If you were to pitch a feature, what might that be and where might you pitch it?

Day 8

Raise your profile and personal brand

Today let's get thinking about some of the ways you can promote yourself and your work that could work even more efficiently to drive sales and a quicker return on time invested in trying to secure print media.

There have never been so many opportunities for founders to become famous. Here are just a few...

Podcasts

Podcasts are a great way to hype yourself to a niche audience. Think back to your communication objectives and which format is good for you. If you enjoy speaking and are time-poor, this could be the perfect medium for you.

They're evergreen content, meaning that they'll continue to be played for a long time. Both my clients and I have been able to pick up new clients, brand partnerships and other types of work from podcasts long after the episode was recorded. It's less about the size of the podcast and more about the audience match.

Tips

- Listen to a few different episodes of what you'd like to pitch for.
- Reference any shows/interviews that particularly moved you.
- Have you written a compelling subject header on your email?
- Show the synergy between your two audiences to demonstrate that you'll be an asset as a guest and can bring an audience to listen.

Guest speaker

Speaking at local, national and international events can be great for your kudos, building brand awareness, creating connections and driving new business. Speaking is usually one of the best ways to bring sales.

Start small

Consider free skill-sharing events in your local community at the beginning. It might not be the sort of thing that raises your profile but it's good for your soul. It's also great practice to get on stage, hold a mic and polish your delivery.

Join some networking groups/attend events

Exploring all the different event opportunities and possibilities that are out there gives you an idea of what works well and what could be improved on. Seeing various presentations will also give you ideas for your own content and style.

Most of the bigger conferences will issue a call for speakers, and some of the biggest ones might invite you to pitch over a portal.

Use Google/ChatGPT to research thoroughly open speaker submissions that can fit for the subjects that you talk about.

Raise your profile and personal brand

Bigger conferences work far in advance

Within one to two months of a large international event finishing, they'll start to open up registration for the next one and for submission for speakers. It's worth registering for these for the reminder.

TedX.com

Check the website for local events or themed events that have been programmed that are relevant to your expertise. Connect with your local TedX producers/programmers and try pitching to them.

Tips

Here are ten top tips from Kate Mander, former Senior Talent Producer for The Stylist Group, for getting on the radar of people who book events:

1. **Email pitches:** Keep them concise. Who are you and what are your credentials? How

would you like to collaborate? Associated links (i.e. your website, showreel).

2. **Examples:** Anecdotal evidence means that I can see them in action and build a better picture of how they could work for our audience.
3. **Preparation:** Do your research. Make sure you understand the audience and what we're about.
4. **Takeaways:** What four things will our audience learn/what are the takeaways from the session?
5. **Invitations:** Invite me along. We work on multiple content all year round and are always looking for new exciting talent to work with.
6. **Instagram:** Connect with me on Instagram. If you're on my radar, it could be I find just the right thing at the right time.
7. **Contact/context:** 100% send me a short bio at the end of your pitch, a contact number, link to your handles and website, but no CVs. I'm after a bespoke pitch, not to hire you.
8. **Tone:** Confident, not cocky – I definitely want to see confidence and I want people to reach out, but get the balance right.

Raise your profile and personal brand

9. **Hype yourself:** Put yourself out there.
10. **Time it right:** *Stylist* Live happens in November and I'm inundated with pitches in the week after that event for the following year. But that's far too soon; we start discussing our content about six months before the event, so that's the time to make contact.

🖉 So what? Over to you...

1. Which podcasts would be a good fit for you? Create a target list and listen to some recent episodes as a first step.

2. What immediate opportunities are there in your local area or specialist field for speaking, and how can you make the most of them?

3. What bigger events or conferences will you aim to target?

Day 9

Being creative ('brain farts')

Brain farts are what I call the creative ideas that can pop into your head.

Perhaps you have an event, launch or other opening that provides you with an opportunity to think beyond just writing a news release or creating a post for social media? As small business owners and solopreneurs, creativity, agility and being able to borrow from big business is our secret weapon. Our best asset is as ourselves as the founder, and thinking about how we could do PR differently and more creatively could help us cut through and go viral. Here are some ideas to get you started.

Being creative ('brain farts')

Newsjacking

This is when you find some news to jack to create your own story. A great recent example of this were all the brands who did something around Taylor Swift playing a concert in their home town. We saw renames, limited edition partnerships, bespoke merchandise.

If you want a few ideas on how to get started on newsjacking, here are five top tips from Sophie Raine, formerly deputy MD of W Communications. They're based on how an agency approaches this for its clients, and you can adapt them for yourself as a small business owner:

1. Adopt a *conversation first* mindset. Focus on existing conversations happening among consumers and within the media.
2. Mine your business for stories. Look at what existing collateral you have that we could build stories from.
3. Find natural 'moments' across the calendar for your brand. There are plenty of news hooks and talking points throughout the year.
4. Identify your audiences' influences. If you find this out, you can pitch in the right place.

5. Keep your eyes and ears open. Have a natural thirst for news, an eye on new trends and the ability to consume and enjoy media in all forms.

NB. It isn't about just getting into traditional press; you can use these moments, for example, to mock up an artificial intelligence image on your social media feed to create a fun engagement moment.

Tips

- Remember that you only have a short window to newsjack; make sure you have time to be reactive so that you can see it all the way through.
- Make sure you have a reason to be in that space and you're not hijacking. International Women's Day is a classic to see brands jumping on, many of whom don't have a right to be there.
- Don't waste a big budget on a newsjacking stunt. As a small agile business, you're in a place to test out as many of these as you can on a budget.

Being creative ('brain farts')

Picture stories

Have you ever considered a picture story? I love a picture story but have found most small business owners haven't considered this a tool they can use.

Every single publication has a picture editor and is looking for news stories in pictures on a daily basis. You can either specifically create a picture story or consider how you could use pictures to maximize your story.

The DOs

- Your picture should answer any three of these: who, what, why, when and where?
- You should be able to tell what the story is without much explaining.
- Include human interest?
- Make sure you take a range of story shots.
- Make sure you have a range (six to ten) of landscape and portrait images that goes in your final edit.
- Embed a caption that tells the story of your image and include a credit to your photographer.
- Name your image.

The DON'Ts

- Your picture should not be an advertisement.
- Don't take a picture for a timely occasion and then try to bank it for the following week. You need to issue the picture the same day for news.
- Don't issue too many choices to picture editors or picture desks – too much choice is overwhelming.

Ways to use picture stories

Work with a picture agency. This is the more expensive way but there's a good chance your image will be put on the newswires, which means it goes to every picture desk editor across the country. The photographers that they send for your job are also experts in telling stories via photos so will come with their own ideas to help sell your story.

Create your own photo story. If you have the budget to pay for your own photography, these are the need-to-know steps to issue a photo story as picture news for national and online media. Quick note: the timings for national picture stories are on a 24-hour cycle (whereas your local paper might only appear weekly).

Being creative ('brain farts')

Identify your picture

Your hero image may change but, before you do the shoot, plan out a few different shots you can take on the day and ensure this tells the story clearly.

Map out your timings

This is the most important part. If it's Monday and you want to be in Tuesday's papers, you need to be shooting ideally before 9:00 am on the Monday morning. That way your photographer has time to turn around the edit. And you can send your shortlist off before midday. It's *highly* unlikely that anything issued outside of newswires after 2:00 pm will make the papers the next day. If your shoot is in the afternoon/evening, it's even less likely to make the next day's print *but* you can still issue for 'pics of the day' as most nationals have online picture carousels and sometimes the weekend papers do a round-up of the best shots of the week.

Prepare your media list

Ensure you have the details of the picture editor *or* the desk you're pitching to. If you're selling a picture story in for the business desk, for example, then you'll need the business reporter. A Google search or phone call to the switchboard should be able to provide you with the generic email address for the desk you need.

Subject line

Ensure your subject line clearly tells the story.

Photocall template

Here's a template that can be used for inviting media for a photo or video call, although obviously the filming/photography options differ between the two.

What:

Where:

Date:

Time:

Then add in a note about what facilities are available; for example, 'Photo, video and interview opportunities available', 'Wi-Fi access available', 'Metered street parking available', etc.

About paragraph:

Being creative ('brain farts')

Write *one* succinct paragraph that explains what the event is about. Consider:

- What makes the picture noteworthy that the photographer can capture?
- Are there any experts, charity representatives, voice of authority, etc., that can be offered for interview?
- Any other succinct points that could be added?

ENDS

For further details, contact [name, email and contact number]:

Editors' notes:

Insert press release or additional information about story here.

When to issue a photocall

I often use a three-prong attack: issue a few weeks in advance to make sure it's in the diary and sent in advance, follow up a week in advance and then call the day before to remind them/see if anyone is coming.

Exclusive option

By offering exclusive access to an event, you might be taking a risk, but if they do decide to go through with it and the picture takes off, this can go viral.

Research

I personally *love* a research story, but as they involve a lot of work, they're not for those who are risk averse. The reality is that you often have one bite of the cherry to get your research covered by national news and if you pitch in on a busy news day you won't get a look-in (like the time I phoned the Press Association to see if they were interested in my news story and at just that minute it had been announced Osama bin Laden had been captured – story over).

There are two options for research stories:

1. Create your own research
2. Work with a research partner

Here are some good reasons for using a research partner:

- They'll help you pull out the sort of headlines and then questions that are interesting.

Being creative ('brain farts')

- By starting with headlines, everyone can think about what's newsworthy, what might have already been done or how we could take the story on.
- Once you agree the headlines, you can work backwards to then craft your questions.
- Your questions then go into the field and after a period of time you get the raw data back.
- You can use the answers to develop a press release or news angle.
- Using ONS population statistics you can create some very media-worthy headlines beyond the people you've polled, as long as your segmentation is good enough (e.g. if 20% of your correspondents believe something, then you can take 20% of the ONS population statistics to, say. '13 million people think', etc.).

Tips

- If you're doing a poll you need at least 1,000 respondents to be credible.
- Ideally, you need to have 2,000 respondents nationwide to get a national news story.
- If you want to pitch a story to broadcast, you need a minimum of 3,000 correspondents.

Business book

Part of my mission is to support as many small businesses as possible with their publicity, and writing a book fully supports this. It will help you to:

- Raise your industry profile.
- Secure paid-for speaking opportunities.
- Become a teacher/lecturer in your industry.
- Have ambitions to sell coaching, courses or workshops.

You can either self-publish or you can seek a business publisher, but whichever option you take, you do need to write a book proposal to get clear on who you're writing for and your distinctive approach.

Here are a few of the opportunities I had following the announcement that I was writing a book:

- I was invited to speak on multiple podcasts as a PR expert and the book deal was always something I was asked about.
- I was paid to host panels and workshops.
- I generated email sign-ups with people registering for further information about the book.
- I secured multiple guest post slots for the six months in the run-up to the book being published as well as event invitations for

book signings and speaking post-launch to continue to drive momentum.

Tips

- Spend time thinking about your book, read other business books from your area and think about what you like and don't like.
- Think about how your book can be used as a promotional tool to deliver for your business.
- Make sure the book is fully aligned with what you want to do as a business. I want to be seen as a PR expert for small businesses. My book helps me do exactly that.

So what? Over to you…

1. Take a look at today's news: is there a story you can newsjack? How?

Being creative ('brain farts')

2. Give it a try: write your newsjack story and post on social media.

3. What opportunities do you have for picture and/or video stories over the next few weeks?

Day 10

Non-traditional PR

While traditional media forms are still important, there's a range of newer possibilities to consider as part of your PR mix.

Influencer engagement

For businesses with little to no budget, working effectively with influencers can have a transformative effect on visibility and sales.

Influencer marketing is the term used for working with individuals with an engaged and higher following on social media platforms. When you work with the right influencer, you gain access to their friends, fans and audience who in theory should also be your target audience, and this endorsement automatically catapults your brand from an unknown entity into something positive and desirable.

- *Build relationships directly* – where you contact the influencer yourselves.
- *Work with a talent agency* – when you have a budget and want to pay the influencer to promote your product.
- *Work with a talent platform* – where you might have a larger pot that you can carve up across multiple influencers.

Tips for implementing a successful influencer marketing campaign

Research

Do your homework! Come up with a list of experts, personalities or organizations you want to reach out to. Cross-reference this against your business objectives – are these people going to have an influence on your brand's target audience?

Ego check

Think about people that might benefit from you, your product and service and maybe pick a range

Non-traditional PR

to see who and what is a driver for you. Test out both nano-influencers (fewer than 5,000 followers) and micro-influencers (5,000–100,000 followers). Chances are they have a very engaged audience *and* they'll be grateful and honoured to work with you.

Often when we try to work with celebrities or people with a huge audience, they'll command huge fees and might not be a great audience match.

Participation and appreciation

Engage with everyone, big and small – see how they get engagement and how they add value, and think about how you can do the same. How about gifting? A guest takeover? A collaborative live video?

What success looks like to you

Track your numbers before you do a campaign and, on a basic level, track immediate traffic and as many stats as possible, such as sales, engagement and followers after the campaign.

Don't pay over the odds

If someone comes back to you with an influencer/ brand deck, check them out. There are many free tools online to check engagement levels and costs per post.

Pick your niche wisely

Can you dare to be different and go to a different space with your USP?

How to use social media platforms

I'm not asking you to be active on every single social media platform but I'd recommend the following:

- Have what I call a shop window or menu on each social media platform. Include an up-to-date biography and headshot with your one-liner.
- Include a pinned post at the top that sets out the ways people can work with you.
- Don't have more than three ways of working. For me, it's buying my books, subscribing to my newsletter or booking me for one-to-one mentoring.
- I also do guest writing, teaching, speaking and content creation, but too much information and too many choices quickly become overwhelming, so stick with the essentials.

- Each platform has its own requirements, challenges and opportunities to consider…

X/Twitter

X, formerly known as Twitter, is still the best free resource to connect with media and understand what they're looking for. Search the hashtag #journorequest, select 'latest', and you'll see a steady stream of journalists looking for spokespeople, case studies or businesses for interview.

X/Twitter lists

Information overload is common! I've found that using X/Twitter lists is an essential part of keeping track of just a few tailored groups that are bespoke to me and my business.

What are lists? Think of them like aspirational WhatsApp chat groups. I have a few lists:

- *Cool venues*: I always like to follow new spaces that are opening up and get a feel for the sort of events they're showcasing. It's like brand food.
- *Start-up journalists*: these are the journalists that, whatever the client, I need to know inside

out. The articles they share give me an idea of what's currently topical. And I can see when they're looking for ideas and contributors.
- *Innovative businesses*: to be an expert, you need to constantly be evolving and learning; therefore, keeping an eye on what other brilliant businesses are doing helps to keep me and the businesses I work with on their toes.
- *New journalists*: I have a private list of new contacts I've made and want to build a relationship with, to remind me these are the people I need to build engagement with.

Instagram

Journalists are increasingly using Instagram to get a quick snapshot of what a business is about. I'd advise a word of caution, though, about sending unsolicited DMs to personal Instagram accounts of media on Instagram. Instead, focus more on using Instagram as a billboard for getting the attention for brand collaborations, bookings for speaking and podcast requests.

At the top, have a pinned post of ways to work with me and make the most of highlights to show press coverage, client wins, different strands of work. If you're not posting all the time, at least make sure that if someone has a quick glance at your grid they'll immediately know what you're about.

Facebook

Networking groups are without doubt the most helpful *free* resources and advice I've gleaned for myself and for a lot of my clients. I've already mentioned Charlotte Crisp's Lightbulb paid Facebook group for connecting with press and there are many more similar for podcasts, freelance writing, speaking, etc.

Local/regional groups

An underused resource is local Facebook groups. They're a great way to connect and cross-collaborate with other businesses in your local area to grow your platform.

Facebook Stories

Getting traction on your Facebook newsfeed is very difficult, but with every social media channel looking to grow into publishers, video content will take precedence, so try to share as much on stories as possible.

LinkedIn

A lot of small businesses ignore LinkedIn as a platform because they identify their audience as a particular consumer and see LinkedIn as a B2B (business-to-business) channel. Here are a few reasons why I think small businesses need to take LinkedIn seriously:

- Opportunities to be selected to work for bigger brands.
- If you're looking to make alternative income from your expertise, then producers, event bookers, brand partners all look out for great talent on this platform.
- Taking people on the behind-the-scenes journey of your business encourages sign-ups and sales.
- You can now follow connections such as journalists or marketing partners to keep abreast of their content and build your relationships with them.
- It's a helpful focus group tool – when I was choosing my book cover, my network and

then their network all provided really useful feedback. Asking genuine questions will drive engagement with your profile as well as provide useful feedback.

TikTok

Despite what you might think, TikTok isn't just for viral dancing videos for the kids. For small business owners it's a fantastic way to take people behind the scenes, and you don't have to create videos, you can simply show photos in a carousel.

If you're braver, it's a much easier way to create rough-and-ready, authentically human content, and you have a great chance of getting exposure as the 'For You' algorithm that brings content to users' attention is more democratic than that used on many other platforms.

So what? Over to you…

1. How can *you* connect effectively with journalists on social media?

2. Which platform is your business's 'home' and how can you make more of an impact there?

3. If you were to write a business book to showcase your expertise, what might that look like?

All the other days: Onwards and upwards

I know what it's like as a small business owner. Most of the time we're firefighting on the day-to-day, and once you've read this book and started to take action it's hard to keep checking in. But consistency and persistence are key if you want your PR to make a difference. So how do you keep going and keep getting better?

If nothing else, try to set some time aside monthly to review your PR activities and track what's working. Once you know that, you can double down on the promotional activities that work best for you.

Here's a suggested outline for that monthly review...

Review your PR plan

- Where are you in relation to your business goals?

- What has worked well? Did any piece of press activity particularly stand out?
- What hasn't worked so well, and what can you do to rectify this?
- What single thing can you do today that will benefit your long-term communications plan?
- What's happening in six weeks, three months, six months that you need to action?

Media toolkit in action

- Is your biography up to date across all social channels?
- Do you need new press photography or a little refresh?
- Does your photography still fit you?
- Do you need to revise your pitches for guest posts?
- What do you want to be talking about in the next few months?

Press office – traditional

- Have you regularly been checking #journorequest, #haro and/or Lightbulb for

journalists looking for stories that you can respond to?
- What successes have you had? Have you shared them across your own marketing channels?
- Have you kept all networking contacts warm?
- Did you try a new pitch format such as a guest post or feature pitch?
- What are the names of three journalists you could try to build a relationship with?

Personal brand – profile

- Have you set a target for podcasts, guest newsletters or public speaking?
- How many have you achieved?
- What was the feedback?
- Have you secured enough guest panels, posts, competitions, partnerships?
- Have you attended enough events?
- Have you written your newsletter/blog posts?

Creativity and promotional gaps

- Do you have any holes in your calendar that could do with some promotional activity?

- Do you have an opportunity to try something different, such as a picture story or research?

Social media

- Which channels are driving the business growth around your business objectives?
- Which types of posts had the biggest engagement?
- Which types of posts gave you the biggest sales?
- Is your biography and 'ways to work with me' post pinned at the top of every platform?

So what? Over to you...

1. What's been the biggest learning you've taken from this book?

2. How will you make sure that you take these ideas forward?

3. How will you build in regular reviews to keep your PR activity on track?

Conclusion

I hope that this book has shown you the value of no-nonsense PR and how, for nothing more than the cost of your time, you too could make significant growth in your business.

If you're still in any doubt, I hope that showing you how I've created my own lifestyle business using the art of hyping alone demonstrates that it's an effective mechanism.

If I could give you one piece of advice, it's that good PR is more than just about telling your story once – it's the narrative thread that should underpin all your business activity and to keep consistent with this you must treat yourself like your most important client.

Even sat in my garden office at home, I'm still hyping myself through the expertise I share on social channels, the connections I'm following up with, the guest posts I'm writing, the newspapers and magazines I regularly read. Knowing who you are, what your business is about and why you do

Conclusion

it is essential groundwork for building a strong communications programme.

Please follow me on whatever your preferred social channel is – on @lucywernerpr to hear my latest hints, tips and tricks to Hype Yourself, or sign up for our newsletter. If you have any questions, success stories or tips to share with me, please tag me.

Keep on hyping.

Lucy x

Enjoyed this?
Then you'll love…

Hype Yourself: A no-nonsense PR toolkit for small businesses by Lucy Werner

Business Book Awards 2021 Shortlisted Title

A toolkit designed for small businesses, packed with industry secrets from a PR professional that will teach you how to be your own best publicist.

> 'In an industry rife with jargon and snake oil, Lucy demystifies the dark arts of PR and cuts to the chase showing founders everywhere how to get the word out faster, more authentically and without a massive price tag. An essential read for anyone who wants to build a strong profile for their business or themselves.' – Jeff Taylor, Editor in Chief, Courier Media

Enjoyed this? Then you'll love...

'Every small business should take its reputation seriously, and Hype Yourself is a fantastic hands-on guide for business managers up and down the country. If you're looking for a practical book to help you manage your own PR, look no further.' – Francis Ingham, Director General, PRCA

'Covering so much more than just PR, Hype Yourself is a must-read for any business owner wanting to build awareness in an authentic and genuine way. This book cuts the fluff and gives you straight-talking PR advice that you can action before you plough any more time or money into PR. Lucy's thinking is outside the traditional PR box: refreshing and inspiring.' – Rosie Davies-Smith, Founder of PR Dispatch & LFA

Lucy Werner helps founders get famous. She's the founder of The Wern, a PR & design consultancy for startups, and HypeYourself.com, an online DIY platform for small businesses to learn how to build their brand and do publicity for themselves.

She has taught hundreds of entrepreneurs through workshops and talks for Cass Business School, *Courier* magazine, Hatch Enterprise, UAL &

UCL, and has written two bestselling books, *Hype Yourself* and *Brand Yourself*. Named a Startups 21 most influential women of 2021 and The Dots 100 Rising Stars two years in a row, she's also an Adobe Express global ambassador and Domestika instructor.

Other 6-Minute Smarts titles

Write to Think (based on *Exploratory Writing* by Alison Jones)

Do Change Better (based on *How to be a Change Superhero* by Lucinda Carney)

How to be Happy at Work (based on *My Job Isn't Working!* by Michael Brown)

Mastering People Management (based on *Mission: To Manage* by Marianne Page)

Present Like a Pro (based on *Executive Presentations* by Jacqui Harper)

Look out for more titles coming soon! Visit www.practicalinspiration.com for all our latest titles.